SECRETS
TO
MANIFESTING

SECRETS TO MANIFESTING

How to make all your dreams come true

Emily Anderson

SIRIUS

SIRIUS

This edition published in 2023 by Sirius Publishing, a division of
Arcturus Publishing Limited,
26/27 Bickels Yard, 151–153 Bermondsey Street,
London SE1 3HA

ISBN: 978-1-3988-2608-3
AD010770UK

Printed in China

CONTENTS

Introduction

M ANIFESTING IS ABOUT using the power of your mind and emotions to create the life of your dreams. By focusing your thoughts and actions on creating positive feelings, and living from a state of joy, happiness and abundance, you can attract more uplifting experiences and blessings into your world. It is life lived according to the law of attraction, where *like attracts like,* also called the law of mirroring, where everything in your life is a reflection of your vibrational frequency. This fundamental law of nature is based on ancient knowledge that grew popular via the New Thought Movement, which begin in the 1800s (more on this shortly). Awareness of it has expanded in the last couple of decades to include thousands of books, videos and courses by manifesting experts all over the world.

The basic idea is that 'thoughts become things' and what you focus on you attract. Through positive thought, intentions and emotions you align your energy with that of the loving, expansive universe so you can receive the gifts it has for you. These are not just material items such as a beautiful home or a flash new car, but a way of living a richer, deeper, happier life full of meaning, love and prosperity. The key is learning how to feel *as if* your best life has already manifested, then allowing it to unfold by being present enough to see the path you need to follow to get there.

By focusing your attention on how you want to feel when your ideal home, vibrant health or lucrative career manifests, you are raising your vibrational frequency to match that of the benevolent and abundant universe. When you're an energetic match to Source (or God, the Goddess, the Universe, whatever you want to call the deep, expansive power at the heart of all

Creation) you can co-create together to bring your very best self into being and manifest your best life.

But what would this even look like? This book will help you get clear on what it is you would really like to happen in your life. Do you want to get fitter, have lots of loving friends, live in a spacious home by the sea with an organic veggie plot? Would you be happiest running a retreat centre, writing blogs, starting your own business? Think about all the various aspects of your life and what you dream of doing with your time. Envisage the very best outcome for your career, wellbeing and relationships. Dream up all the fabulous things you want to experience so that you can fulfil your highest potential. Allow all the ideas and inspiration to come to you about what would really light you up to do, be and have. Then hand that all over to the Universe, work on keeping your vibe high, and trust that the right things will manifest for you at the right time.

Of course, there are methods for doing this most effectively, including creative visualization, saying affirmations and making vision boards, all of which are explained in this book. Plus, there are issues that can get in the way of manifesting, such as negative thought patterns and conflicting beliefs, which need to be thoroughly examined so that you can fully utilize the ancient secrets of creating your best life.

THE HISTORY OF THE NEW THOUGHT MOVEMENT

It's long been believed that our thoughts are powerful enough to create our reality. After all, everything humans have created started life as a thought in someone's mind. Thinkers and writers in ancient Christian, Hindu and Buddhist scriptures spoke of our thoughts being able to shape our world, and that what we give, we receive similar in return. The Buddha (563–483BCE) wanted people to know that, 'All that we are is a result of what we have thought.' While Jesus taught, 'Believe and you shall receive,' and in the Bible, Proverbs 23:7, it says, 'As a man thinketh in his heart so is he.'

The great Roman emperor Marcus Aurelius said, 'Our life is what our thoughts make it.' In fact, many of the greatest artists, scientists and philosophers of old knew about the law of attraction, including Plato and Socrates, Shakespeare, Beethoven, Newton, Edison and Einstein. Napoleon is quoted as saying, 'Whatever the mind of man can conceive and believe, it can achieve.'

But it wasn't until the early 19th century that these ideas were expanded into the New Thought movement by a series of (mostly American) writers and pioneers of positive thinking whose work has led to the modern law of attraction teachings. These reached many more people with the help of the book and film of *The Secret*, featuring channellers Esther and Jerry Hicks and publisher Louise Hay, whose catalogue of authors from Dr Wayne Dyer and Robert Holden to Gabrielle Bernstein and Kyle Gray are some of the biggest teachers of New Thought today.

The founder of the movement is widely seen as American inventor Phineas Quimby (1802-1866) after his work on psychosomatic illness and the ability to affect your wellbeing with your thoughts. He discovered that excitement could dull pain, and so began a lengthy study into the significant ways that the mind affects the body, including the detrimental impact of negative and false beliefs about oneself.

Around the same time, the controversial Russian-born psychic, medium and spiritual teacher Madame Helena Blavatsky (1831-1891) was travelling the world sharing her skills and wisdom about life's mysteries. Her most influential book, *The Secret Doctrine,* explained that, 'The Universe is worked and guided from within outwards,' and explored the notion that we are who we believe we are, that our self-perceptions influence our reality and identity, and that our thoughts can change our future for the better.

Developing Quimby's theories, American author Prentice Mulford (1834-1891) wrote in depth about his own and others' experiences of the law of attraction in action. His books, including *Thoughts Are Things, The Gift of Understanding,* and *Your Forces and How to Use Them,* form the basis of contemporary law of attraction principles, whereby we can affect not only our health but also life opportunities and material gains with our thinking.

Towards the end of the 19th century and into the 20th, various authors published books popularizing and developing these ideas, including Wallace

D. Wattles' *The Science of Getting Rich,* which first revealed the use of creative visualization, imagining all your dreams in detail to bring them into being. One of the most prolific writers in the New Thought movement, William Walker Atkinson (1862-1932), stumbled across law of attraction ideas when work-stress as a lawyer led to his mental and physical collapse. Inspired by the movement, he launched a New Thought magazine, started a school for mental science, and wrote over a hundred books, including *Thought Vibration: The Law of Attraction in the Thought World.* Often drawing on Hindu teachings about willpower, concentration and personal magnetism, his work introduced the concept of raising our vibrational frequency through our thoughts and actions in order to attract positive experiences and success.

At the same time, Charles Haanel (1866-1949) was also developing ideas of attracting abundance and prosperity through the power of positivity in his books *The New Psychology* and *The Master Key System*. He gave practical techniques to master visualization and cultivate an optimistic and generous mindset to boost your chances of not only financial success, but a happy and fulfilling life all round.

Another bestselling New Thought author was Illinois-born Ralph Waldo Trine (1886-1958), who strongly believed that positive thinking could transform your life if you worked at it with specific techniques and daily habits. His work inspired another writer, journalist Oliver Napoleon Hill, whose hugely successful book *Think and Grow Rich,* published in 1937, has now been made into a film starring Bob Proctor, one of the experts in *The Secret* movie. Hill's book examined the habits of over 500 self-made millionaires in America, including motor industry pioneer Henry Ford and billionaire steel magnate Andrew Carnegie. His research showed that often expectation – of struggle, success or unlimited potential – played a large part in what happened in your life. Positive visualizations also helped build a successful life; as Hill said, 'If you do not see riches in your imagination, you will never see them in your bank balance.'

Having learned from Hill's work, another American writer, William Clement Stone (1902-2002), went on to emphasize that we can only achieve what we desire as long as we are confident in our ability to do so. His motivational phrase, 'If you think you can, do,' led to him taking full advantage of all opportunities that came his way to make him a popular self-help author and philanthropist. Having come from a family seriously in debt from his father's gambling losses, he brought forth the idea that our difficulties, and even traumas, can be used as stepping stones for success. He explained that with the perspective of gratitude for the experience, rather than feeling like a victim, life could be transformed into something more positive. Cultivating an 'attitude of gratitude' remains one of the key ways to manifest greater things, shared especially by contemporary motivational writers and speakers who came after these pioneers, including Gabrielle Bernstein, Dr Joe Dispenza and Dr Wayne Dyer, as well as celebrities such as Oprah Winfrey, Denzel Washington and Jim Carrey.

Building on the concepts of the New Thought writers above, Dyer wrote *Your Erroneous Zones,* published in 1976, his first of over 40 books including *Manifest Your Destiny, Excuses Begone* and *Change Your Thoughts, Change Your Life*, about transforming negative thoughts to turn your life around. Dyer used key spiritual principles for himself to build his hugely successful writing and speaking career from humble beginnings. Not long after, in 1984, Louise Hay released her book *You Can Heal Your Life,* which linked ill health to negative self-talk and unexpressed emotions, and a path out of victimhood to happiness via positive affirmations and self-love. Hay started her own publishing company off the back of her book's success, leading to countless other manifesting books being published, helping people change their thinking and their lives according to the law of attraction.

But it was the Rhonda Byrne book and film *The Secret,* released in 2000, that really piqued the public's appetite for learning how to manifest a better life. It shared so many different experts' tips for attracting prosperity, good health and happiness that their wisdom couldn't be ignored. Highly acclaimed writers Mike Dooley and Bob Proctor; Michael B Beckwith, founder of the Agape International Spiritual Center in California; motivational author, speaker and life coach Jack Canfield; and channeller Esther Hicks are all still tireless in their sharing of the law of attraction secrets to a successful, happy and fulfilled life. Esther and her now deceased husband Jerry wrote many books about the law of attraction, including *Ask and It Is Given*, after they received channelled messages from Source energy, which the pair called Abraham. Now, Esther travels the world sharing this same wisdom from Source under the name Abraham-Hicks.

THE POWER OF YOUR THOUGHTS

All of the knowledge above explains that thoughts are a powerful force, influencing everything from our health and wellbeing to our relationships and careers. Our mind works like a magnet, attracting more of the same thoughts and images. Positive thoughts can raise your energy, make your day go well, and help you have a happy life. On the other hand, negative thinking can bring you down, make you unwell and create situations that might have been avoided had your perspective been different.

Try thinking different thoughts now and see how they make you feel. Say something like, 'I'm an idiot,' 'I'm rubbish at this' or 'I'm so tired,' and you'll feel your energy drop and your mood lower. If you continually berate yourself and others in your mind, repeatedly tell yourself a negative story about how life is, nothing will change for the better. You'll feel low vibrations such as depression, anger, jealousy or resentment, and your day will go from bad to worse. Whereas if you tell yourself, 'I am so blessed,' 'I can do this' or 'I am healthy and full of vitality,' you'll find yourself uplifted, confident and capable of seeing and saying yes to more of the opportunities that present themselves on your path. Having a positive outlook helps raise your whole energetic frequency to higher level, which is how you want to be feeling more and more, to match the high vibration of all the wonderful experiences, people and things you long to manifest.

But it's not just about having an upbeat attitude; you also have to believe that change is possible and that you really can have everything you dream of. All the experts are certain that *what you believe, you shall receive*. So your deeper beliefs need exploring to make sure they're in alignment with what you want. Conflicting, limiting beliefs can create blocks to your manifesting capabilities, and will be explored more in Chapter 5 to help you release any negative thinking habits.

Everything begins with our thoughts, and from them our words and actions unfold, taking us on the journey of our life where thoughts become things. The aim is to become more conscious of your thoughts, choosing them wisely, rather than letting them roam wildly, often in a detrimental way to your mental wellbeing, causing obstacles to total bliss and fulfilment. For when your thoughts, words and actions are all aligned towards making your dreams come true, anything is possible.

This book will help you get clear on how to think better thoughts, to make yourself feel better, happier and more fulfilled as you bring your best self into being. It will guide you over any stumbling blocks and setbacks so you don't have to let life's twists and turns keep you in victimhood when you can use the power of your mind to make the best of your life and rise to greater heights. With some effort, focus, imagination and lots of fun, you can start living your most exciting, fulfilling, high-vibe life – now.

CHAPTER 1

Attract better

OVER THE LAST couple of centuries, science has proven that the power of thought can change reality. The great physicist Albert Einstein demonstrated that the act of observing an experiment can change the results. The observer's thoughts, expectations and assumptions about how the experiment will play out have the power to affect the test itself. So the mind of the observer shapes whatever it is perceiving, which means our minds affect, even create, our world. More recently, the work of Bruce Lipton has shown that our minds affect not only our mental and emotional states but our physical health in every way, healing the body of chronic conditions and injuries through the power of belief. His extensive research proves that we are not just a product of our biology, genetics and DNA; we are, in fact, what we believe.

Quantum physicist Max Planck (1858–1947) said, 'When you change the way you look at things, the things you look at change.' So, how we see reality is how reality is for us. It's all about our perception and beliefs, via the thoughts we think. We make our own luck through the power of our mind. What an incredible realization – that we are all able to make our lives literally anything we want. It's the secret that the wealthy leaders of our world have always known, without question. They think thoughts of success and abundance, dream confidently of doing well, and don't let any other thoughts contradict the dominant ones of prosperity. They know that they will succeed at whatever they do to create wealth, and that's exactly what happens. This is the law of attraction in action, where *thoughts become things*.

Thoughts have their own power and act according to certain principles. As one of the original New Thought writers, Prentice Mulford, said, 'Every thought of yours is a real thing — a force.' That force is so powerful, it can manifest what you think about. Many experts, over the ages, agree that once a thought has been thought it has its own power to manifest into physical reality or to attract more similar thoughts or things. It's as if each thought has its own mission to manifest in the world of its thinker.

So if you keep having thoughts about some material thing or other, those things will, at some point, come into your life. If you keep having thoughts about some event or situation happening, then you will see those circumstances start to play out in your life. All of this is down to your thoughts, as long as you don't have conflicting beliefs about manifesting whatever it is. Opposing thoughts get in the way of our dreams coming into reality. So it makes sense to choose what you think about carefully and consciously.

We have a choice about which reality we want to manifest, so why would we choose anything but a brilliant, joyful, fulfilling life? All it takes is your imagination to conjure up the details and feel the positive emotions of it all manifesting. Then you must act upon the urges, signs and inspiration pulling you towards your dreams unfolding in alignment with Source. Source energy's purpose is to expand and become more self-aware. You are a part of this energy, the universal consciousness, life force, or God: it is not something external to you but it *is* you, what created you and what continues to create your life. As a fragment of this life force, you having desires and those desires manifesting is how the universe expands and becomes more aware of itself. So, the universe wants you to achieve whatever it is you dream of, so that it can expand exponentially through your experiences and creations.

BELIEFS MATTER

The only things getting in the way of your thoughts manifesting into your much-desired things or situations are your conflicting beliefs and expectations. These are, once again, thought-based. As Abraham-Hicks says, 'A belief is just a thought you keep thinking.' Whatever you think consistently about yourself, other people, your health, wealth and the world is what shapes your beliefs – and those beliefs create your life.

Motivational author and speaker Dr Wayne Dyer turned the usual phrase 'seeing is believing' around to the more truthful and powerful, *'believing is seeing.'* He explains in many of his books that what you believe to be possible, or not, is what creates your world for you. Your beliefs can limit your life or see it expand to greater heights, put the brakes on any deep desires for fulfilment or see all your dreams manifest.

If your life is staying pretty much the same as it always has, then you're probably thinking the same thoughts you've always thought, and nothing will really change. You have to examine and change your beliefs to make sure they're in alignment with your desires. Otherwise, you may be longing for a partner, for example, but if you ultimately don't trust people or think you're unlovable, it simply won't manifest. Or it will happen, but not in the way you really want. (More on changing your beliefs for the better in Chapter 5.)

Remember, your mind is like a magnet and will attract what you think about. So if you keep focusing on problems or irritations, more of these will be brought into your reality. Instead, appreciate what is working in your life and all the things you enjoy. This includes everything from small daily pleasures, such as having a cup of coffee in the sunshine, enjoying your morning shower, to going for a walk in nature listening to birdsong, to paying more attention to the loved ones in your life and celebrating the wins at work or home.

Focusing on the good stuff already going on in your life is the best way to manifest even better experiences. This is because the thoughts you are having create a frequency, and if you're thinking more positive thoughts and feeling good about things, that creates a higher frequency than if you're complaining, finding fault or feeling negative about your life. This doesn't mean that negative thoughts are necessarily 'bad' and that you should ignore them. Often, they are clues to deeper emotional wounding that still needs to be explored, felt and released with love. But when 'like attracts like' in the realm of thoughts, you want to ensure your mind stays locked on all the loveliness already around you. Feeling a sense of gratitude and appreciation for what's going well, right now, is key to raising your frequency and bringing more joy into your life. This book will explain more secrets to help you.

RAISE YOUR VIBRATION

Your body and mind work like a powerful antenna, beaming out the frequency of your thoughts and feelings. Whatever frequency you attune yourself to, the law of attraction will bring things of the same frequency to you with its *like attracts like* or mirroring principle. To have good things happen to you and attract the situations, people and events of your dreams, you need to consistently feel good and not allow worry over the future or reliving past events drag your energy down. Do all you can to heal from any past traumas, getting all the support you need in the form of therapists or time to reflect and forgive, but don't let your past affect your present, as this will keep it playing out in the future. Raise your frequency by tuning in more to the authentic you underneath all the pain and hurt, so your inner light can shine and your very being become a magnet to the good stuff of life.

Quantum physics proves that everything emits an energy, a vibration. The Hertz Vibration Scale reveals the different levels of vibration emitted by different feelings, created by different thoughts. At the lower end of the spectrum, radiating low-frequency energy, as you might expect, are emotions such as shame, guilt, depression and fear. These are not 'bad' feelings, they just emit a lower vibration than higher-vibe feelings such as appreciation, love, joy and peace (see the full scale on pages 71-2). The key to attracting more of the things that bring you peace, joy and love in your life is to think thoughts that create those feelings. Then you are raising your vibration to match the level of positive feelings you want to have more of in your life.

If thinking happy thoughts isn't quite enough to get you into this higher state of being, the key is to *do something* to bring those emotions about. Ask yourself, 'What will make me feel more alive right now?' It could be anything you enjoy doing, from dancing and singing to petting your dog, hugging your child, cooking, eating a delicious and nutritious meal, or going for a walk or run in nature. Any exercise or activity that puts a smile on your face and makes you feel good about yourself will raise your vibration. But beware of it becoming an addictive distraction from any negative feelings that need to be felt and released. If you're covering up painful feelings by binge drinking or shopping, or even by doing seemingly spiritual activities such as meditation or yoga, but the negative feelings are still unaddressed, they will come out eventually. It's better to face any hurt or pain when it arises. Release the emotions you need to by having a good cry or shout into your pillow, for example, forgiving yourself and others for any pain caused, and then pivoting to a purely positive activity to boost your mood.

Tuning your vibration to happiness is called 'getting into the vortex' by Esther Hicks when she channels Source energy known to her as Abraham. The advice is simply to discover what brings you joy and do more of it so your frequency stays high and you gain some momentum in the direction of your dreams of a better life.

* Make a list of at least ten of your favourite activities and do a few of them every day. Whenever you feel your mood dip, do one of the uplifting things on the list, or at least spend some time thinking about it to raise your energy. Don't feel guilty about taking some time for yourself – that's the low-vibe energy you want to avoid. You are worth spending at least an hour a day on, doing things that make you happy. It's an essential part of not only your self-care routine but also your manifestation practice, so you can attract more situations into your life to boost your wellbeing even more.

ALIGN WITH SOURCE ENERGY

An essential way of raising your vibration to the higher frequencies of peace, love and enlightenment is through meditation. A daily practice of sitting still, eyes closed, and quieting the mind is the best way to stop any negative thoughts in their tracks. Through regular meditation you become able to observe your thoughts as they enter your mind, and let them go more easily, instead of getting attached to them and the emotions they create. Learning to watch your thoughts come and go is the first step to becoming more conscious of what you are creating in your mind, on the path to thinking more positively, more often. Just ten to twenty minutes of meditation per day, to start with, ideally around the same time each day, has so many benefits for mind, body and spirit. It eases anxiety, gives you more energy and boosts your mood. All of which, of course, raises your frequency.

Furthermore, calming your mind enables you to become more aware of the stillness behind all thoughts, the deeper consciousness within you, from which everything unfolds, otherwise known as Source energy, or God, the Goddess, Allah, the Tao or whatever you choose to call it. Tuning into Source through meditation and, as you become more practised at it, throughout the day by being fully present in every moment, raises your vibration to a level of bliss and aligns you with the creative power of the universe, of which you are a part. The more you tap into this expansive, creative energy, this field of oneness, the easier it is to come into alignment with all it wants for you. Meditation is the start of your manifestation journey because what you are doing is bringing into being a new aspect of yourself, which has always been part of you on a spiritual level – your thoughts just got in the way. With regular practice, this aspect of Source will express itself through you, as long as you let it and don't let the ego, the mind's identity of yourself that has been reinforced over time, take over and stop it with false negative beliefs about who you are (see more on breaking through beliefs in Chapter 5).

How to meditate

Make sure you have some uninterrupted time for yourself to meditate, ideally first thing in the morning before the mind starts to race with its to-do list for the day. Ten to twenty minutes is perfect to start with. Eventually, you may end up sitting for half an hour or more, or do it twice a day. You could set a timer with a gentle alarm. But if it's on your phone, be sure to turn it to aeroplane mode so you are not interrupted by any calls or texts.

Find a quiet, comfortable space in your home to sit or kneel, either on cushions, on the floor or on a chair, as long as your spine is upright and you won't feel the need to fidget. You may want a blanket for your legs, or a shawl for your shoulders, to stay warm and cosy.

You can light a candle, or some incense, to start the session with an awareness of this being a sacred time for you to connect with yourself, your soul and spirit energy.

Settle down into a comfortable posture, back straight, chin slightly tucked in so your crown and heart chakras are in alignment. Place your hands on your lap, with palms facing upwards in receiving mode.

Softly close your eyes and start to become aware of your breath, breathing regularly in and out of your nose. Feel the air move in your nostrils with each breath.

Now start taking some longer, deeper breaths, really filling your lungs with fresh air, perhaps holding that in-breath for a few seconds, and then releasing that breath and again waiting a few seconds before drawing another breath in. Allow the breath to gently fall into its natural rhythm and let your whole body and mind relax. Become really present in your body. Try placing your awareness on one of the areas mentioned below, such as your third eye chakra or heart centre.

Don't worry if your mind wanders during meditation. This is perfectly natural; it's what the mind does. But when thoughts arise, try not to run with them, starting a narrative going in your head and triggering emotions that go with them. Instead, imagine each thought, as it comes up, turning into a bubble or a cloud and floating away. Or you can label each thought 'thinking' and remind yourself you are meditating now. Pressing thoughts can – and will – return when you are finished. For now, give yourself this gift of a little time to just *be*, calmly sitting, breathing and stilling your thoughts.

At some point in your practice, you may realize that you've not had a single thought for a while, you've just been at one with the Now. Try to elongate this experience as you make this practice a daily habit.

When you have finished meditating, bring your awareness back to your surroundings by feeling the floor beneath you. Rub your palms together and put your palms over your closed eyes. Open your eyes and slowly remove your hands. Take your time going back to your day. Drink some water to ground and refresh you.

How to deepen your connection to your spirit and your soul during meditation

Tune in to your soul by imagining a small sphere of light, six to eight feet above your head, as suggested by spiritual teacher Lee Harris on leeharrisenergy.com. See it shining and floating above you, guiding you from on high. What does your soul want you to know, right now? Ask it pertinent questions, such as:

- ✦ What does my soul want to tell me today?

- ✦ What is emerging in my life now?

- ✦ What will I create next in my life?

- ✦ What would I really like to manifest in my life?

- ✦ How can I help myself feel good today?

- ✦ What joy am I bringing into my life now?

- ✦ How can I express myself and my dreams more in the world?

To cultivate inner vision and hear the wisdom from your deeper self, bring your awareness to your third eye chakra, right between your eyebrows. This energy centre is the gateway to hearing, feeling and knowing your own inner wisdom.

To listen to the heart and hear what it really wants for you in this lifetime, simply bring your awareness to your heart space in the centre of your chest. Feel a sense of warmth there. Sense or see a big ball of pink light emanating love outwards, filling your whole body. Keep your focus on this ball of love light emanating from your heart, and tune in to what it truly desires.

Gain wisdom from spirit by visualizing a column of bright white light flowing from the heavens into your crown chakra and down into your heart. Feel your heart expand with the light of spirit as it connects with the cosmos. Feel the bliss that bathing in this white light brings. Sit in this field of spirit love light for as long as you wish, and if any guidance comes through, via inspiration or creative urges, note it down afterwards and act on it as soon as you can.

Afterwards, clear your aura by saying, 'I clear my energy field of any energy that is not mine,' after you've connected with spirit in these ways. Ground yourself by feeling the floor beneath you, giving thanks to Mother Earth for supporting you.

Keep a meditation journal to write down how long you spent doing it, how it felt, any difficulties and observations of the practice itself. Record any deeper insights you may have, any guidance from spirit or questions to and answers from your soul, felt during or after meditation as you go about your day.

Spending time just being, watching your breath and stilling your mind, connects you with your soul's urges for full creative expression and expansion. Until you curb your constant thinking, through meditation and mindfulness, paying attention to every sensation, action, thought and feeling as you go about your day, you won't be able to hear what your soul wants for you. It's by connecting with the soul that our deepest desires can come to the fore, rising like bubbles of inspiration in our awareness.

Through the self-discipline and inner strength that daily meditation practice brings, you will gain a certainty in your inner voice and the guidance from spirit showing you the way forward in your life. You will experience an inward sense of your path towards all you desire, along with the power and capability to really go for the life of your dreams.

CHAPTER 2

Clear intentions

MANIFESTING WORKS BEST when the ideas for how you want your life to be come from your own soul, not from what others want for you or what's expected by society. Getting deeply in touch with what your best self wants involves a lot of *being* and allowing things to unfold naturally, not forcing your will if things don't match up. You need to be still enough, often enough, to hear the guidance from spirit and your soul's urges, to notice the signs and synchronicities that will steer you on the correct course to fulfilment, trusting that a higher power knows the way to the best life imaginable.

To hear what your soul wants to manifest, try journalling the answers to certain questions. Give yourself regular, uninterrupted blocks of time with a pen and notebook and write down your first, most instinctive thoughts, or even some lists, about the following:

★ What do you like most about yourself?

★ What activities make you feel happiest?

★ What have you always been interested in?

★ What are you curious to learn more about?

★ What are your natural gifts you'd like to share with the world?

★ What are your top priorities in life?

★ Your wildest desires?

★ Who are the people you admire and why?

★ What are your short-term goals?

★ Your long-term goals?

★ Where do you see yourself in ten years' time?

As you write your answers down, be aware of how each makes you feel. The ones that make you feel exhilarated and alive, that make your heart beat faster with excitement at the thought of doing it, that light you up the most, are the things you need to go for.

DREAM UP YOUR BEST LIFE

Once you start getting ideas for what you want to happen in your life that fill you with passion and excitement, allow yourself to daydream about them. It may have been a punishable offence at school, but now you can use your imagination to dream your desires into being. The brain doesn't actually know the difference between what's real and what's imagined, so, by imagining something intensely enough, your brain thinks it's already happening, and so does your body with the flood of emotions that comes with thinking about it. Then it's just a matter of time before it actually does become reality. Visualize with the positive intention of improving your life and it will manifest.

While it's great to go into the details of exactly what you want, do not make the mistake of trying to work out *how* it will all happen. Leave the specific details of that to the Universe. The main thing to focus on is how you want to feel when all your dreams come to fruition. Allow yourself to imagine yourself in scenes after what you want to happen has happened, dwelling in the feel-good sensations of the success of the end result. It's happiness and fulfilment you're after in all areas of your life, so these are the feelings you need to cultivate with your mind.

If you want to bring a new relationship into your life, spend time thinking about how you want to feel when you're with that amazing person.

Yes, think about the different qualities, looks and traits you'd like them to have, but don't get hung up on wanting a particular person. See yourself in warm, loving hugs and feel the happiness of being in a supportive, fun-filled relationship. Send that feeling out to the universe to match with the right partner.

The same goes for if you want to get a promotion or a new job. Imagine yourself receiving the letter of employment and feel how happy you'll be knowing you've got the job of your dreams. Visualize being praised and congratulated for your work, and feel how ecstatic you would be winning awards, new contracts or clients. Spend time visualizing the end result and leave the *when* and *how* to the Universe.

CREATIVE VISUALIZATION TIPS

★   Spend just five minutes at a time intensely visualizing what you want. Any longer and you can get sidetracked. It needs to be very focused on evoking the emotion of the best possible outcome.

★   Visualize different dreams separately, don't link them together, one coming true dependent on another. For example, starting and running your own successful business, and buying your dream home.

★ Only do it once or twice a day. You need to be primarily appreciating all you have in the present rather than always dreaming about your future. Spending too much time wishing and wanting highlights the gap between where you are and where you want to go. You need to feel good about where you are in order to move forward into an even more fulfilling future (more on appreciation in Chapter 6).

★ Focus on the feelings of happiness, excitement, victory, success, love or abundance that you want to feel as a result of whatever it is you desire. Don't even worry if that's all you do and you can't see the scenes, relationships and experiences that will bring these emotions about; the Universe will take care of that. Just keep on feeling good about whatever is coming in your future.

★ Be gentle and patient with yourself. You will still get anxious about what may or may not happen, or continue to have arguments with friends or family in your mind, even while you're visualizing. But now you'll be able to see it as negative thinking and stop it in its tracks. It's okay, everyone does it, and it can even help to bring stronger desires to the surface as you pivot back to more positive thoughts and visualize experiencing uplifting emotions in your mind.

SETTING INTENTIONS

Once you've dreamed up what your best life looks and feels like, the next step is to start taking action towards it. This is where intention setting comes in, so you can focus your mind on your target, giving yourself the energy and impetus needed to do the tasks that move you closer to your goals.

Set your intentions clearly by writing down whatever comes from deep within your soul or from the yearnings of your heart after writing '*My intention is…*'

Relationship tip

Believe in positive intent in all relationships, including the one with yourself. This way, you become open to feedback to improve your life, rather than taking any comments or actions personally. Set the intention to see all relationships as a chance to learn more about yourself and others, so even criticism is seen from a positive perspective. But not abuse, don't stand for that. And not self-criticism – that needs to stop at once! Always talk kindly to yourself, encourage, celebrate and appreciate everything you do, feel and are. Be your own cheerleader – you deserve it.

First you may want to write freehand all the intentions you have for a better life. For example, to find a fun-loving, supportive life partner, to improve finances, get out of debt, have more vitality, find joy in the little things, travel the world, work on spiritual development and so on. Then, work out which are the most important to you, which to work on now. For these, you can write out individual positive statements of intent, in the form of affirmations (see next page).

The energy transmitted by positive intentions helps you get away from negative thinking habits and more into the power of deep inner guidance, which helps you see and do the work needed to get to where you want to go. A great intention to set before you go to bed at night to stop the train of negativity in your mind comes from Abraham-Hicks:

'I AM THE CREATOR OF MY OWN REALITY AND I LIKE THAT. AS I SLEEP TONIGHT, MOMENTUM IS GOING TO SUBSIDE BECAUSE MY THOUGHTS ARE NOT GOING TO BE ACTIVE AND THE LAW OF ATTRACTION WILL STOP REACTING TO MY THOUGHTS. HOWEVER, IT WILL CONTINUE TO REACT TO THE THOUGHTS OF MY INNER BEING, WHO NEVER SLEEPS. WHEN I WAKE UP, I WILL FEEL THE MOVEMENT OF WHAT MY INNER BEING KNOWS.'

Then when you wake up you will feel more of a pull towards doing the things your inner self wants, to bring you pleasure and enjoyment in life. Your ego mind may try to resist by going back to its negative ways of pushing against what's good for your soul, but you will now be able to see it, stop it and choose to get back on the path to joy and freedom. Try using some of the affirmations below to re-train your brain, and if you still experience resistance, read through Chapter 5 on the challenges you may be facing and how to improve the way your mind works.

AFFIRMATIONS

Affirmations are positive statements of intent to be, feel or act in a certain way, or to have, experience or achieve something in your life. Saying phrases that resonate with you and your intentions regularly can really help manifest what you want. Write your favourites out in your journal to say to yourself daily, put them up in places around your home, such as on your mirror, to say out loud as you get ready for the day, or use them as a centrepiece in a vision board (see next chapter on how to make one) to manifest all you dream of.

While simply saying affirmations can change your perspective and raise your frequency, it is best to be in a neutral to positive place to begin with to help them manifest. So, either say them straight after meditating, so you're coming from a place of peace, or first do or think about something that makes you happy, and then state your intentions for what you desire in your life. This is 'getting into the vortex' according to Abraham-Hicks, where everything you long to manifest is waiting to come to you. You just have to raise your energy to a higher frequency to align with it and stay there as much as you can to attract all the good experiences to you.

All affirmations need to be clear, so no *ifs* or *buts*. Saying them should push you out of your comfort zone a little, but they must ring true for you. If there's any doubtful reaction or internal resistance when you say them, you're sending conflicting messages to the universe and they won't manifest. They want to be formulated in the present tense, as if they are already in existence, so you feel the positive feelings connected to them in the present moment.

So, no *I will* or *I want to* or *I'm going to try,* as these are too vague and set sometime in the future, always just out of reach. *I* statements are best, such as:

I am...   I commit to...

I deserve...   I am open to...

I choose...   I am willing to...

Or:

My body is...   The Universe supports...

My relationships are...

Or, if feeling negative, start your statements with:

I release...   I forgive...

Then state what it is you want along the lines of the suggestions below:

AFFIRMATIONS TO START THE DAY:

Saying affirmations first thing in the morning is a great way to set a positive intention for how the day will unfold and keep your frequency high. You can always say them whenever you feel your energy drop to give you a quick boost.

Today is a wonderful day.

I am excited about today.

I start my day
with positivity and
appreciation.

I am open to exciting
opportunities.

I am receptive to new
experiences.

I allow the Universe to
flow through me today.

I experience life to the
full today, enjoying every
moment.

My day unfolds with ease,
joy and fulfilment.

I allow my soul to lead
the way.

All is well.

I am exactly where I am
meant to be.

FOR IMPROVED HEALTH AND WELLBEING

Appreciate all your body does for you every day, keeping you alive by breathing and beating your heart, enabling you to walk anywhere, to run, dance, swim and stretch. The more you focus on health and vitality, the more your body and mind will respond by feeling healthy, happy and rejuvenated. Say to yourself:

I am well rested and energized.

I choose wholesome, nourishing foods that revitalize me.

My body is healthy and full of vitality.

I am improving my health every day.

I move with ease and enthusiasm.

I can heal anything by healing my beliefs first.

I am powerful and strong.

I choose to feel better each day.

I am a miracle of nature.

I appreciate all my body does for me.

I am happy and I am healthy.

FOR DEEPENING YOUR SPIRITUALITY

Connect deeply to the power of the universe, trusting in Source energy to bring blessings to you easily. Tune in to your soul and spiritual guidance every day by affirming the following:

I am fully supported by the universe.

I am open to receive divine guidance to help me on my path.

Everything is unfolding according to my highest good.

I radiate love and joy wherever I go.

I trust my inner vision and intuition.

I am a being of divine light, full of unlimited potential.

I listen to the voice of my soul every day.

I share my happiness with the world through my smile.

I am guided by my higher self, which always wants the best for me.

I choose to live in love.

FOR MORE MONEY AND PROSPERITY

To attract more money, you have to focus on wealth, abundance and prosperity rather than the lack of these in your life. Tackle debt not by dwelling on it and worrying over it, but by paying it off even a tiny bit at a time. Explore any negative beliefs you have about money and affirm that you are releasing them. Notice the abundance in nature and feel it flowing through you as you say:

I release my negative beliefs around money.

I deserve a fantastic income.

I follow my passions, which leads to prosperity.

I attract more money than I need.

I make an excellent living doing what I love.

I am worthy of a prosperous life.

Money comes to me with ease.

I am wealthy inside and out.

I love money and money loves me.

The universe flows with abundance and brings gifts of prosperity to me.

TO IMPROVE YOUR WORK SITUATION

Even if you don't enjoy your job, try to find something about it to be appreciative of so the universe can give you more of that quality in your next role. Stating what you love about your work or career, and affirming what your gifts are and what work you want to attract, will bring a better job into being. Affirm:

I enjoy being paid for my brilliant ideas and accomplishments.

All my past experiences are leading me to my perfect job.

I love my easy commute / light and airy office / friendly colleagues / respectful boss (whatever resonates most with you about where you work).

I am attracting my ideal job now.

I am ready to experience a fantastic new job where I am fully creative, productive and fulfilled.

I am full of creative potential.

I deserve a fulfilling, well-paid and exciting career.

I attract a highly paid job of my dreams.

I am manifesting the perfect job for me, with the right people to help me thrive.

My positive vibration attracts exciting work opportunities.

FOR AMAZING RELATIONSHIPS

Remember, what you focus on expands. So if you're focusing on a friend's or a partner's less-than-desirable qualities or any arguments, they will manifest more. Whereas if you think of all the things you admire about them or appreciated when you first met, more of their good qualities will become evident. To bring about positive change in relationships say:

I forgive any wrongs and move forwards with love and light.

My relationships are always loving, supportive, joyful and fulfilling.

I forgive myself for thinking negative thoughts about anyone.

I am open to new relationships, perfect for me, and trust they will manifest.

I see the good in others manifest in my life.

It is safe to be myself in
all my relationships.

I feel good about myself,
just as I am.

I deserve to experience
love in my life.

I offer my relationship
grievances up to a higher
power.

I am open to receiving all
the love in the universe.

STOP THINKING ABOUT WHAT YOU DON'T WANT

A terrible trap to get into in life is complaining about what you don't want. If you're always finding fault with what's going on in your world, whether in your head or out loud to others, you're spending too much time focusing on what's going wrong and what you don't want. If you're listening to and sympathizing with someone else telling you their troubles, it's the same focus on what's not wanted. If this becomes your dominant frequency, the universe will simply match it, giving you more situations and scenarios to complain about.

Remember, the universe responds to your frequency and energy flows where attention goes. So if your mind is always wallowing in the worst aspects of your life, that's what will expand, even if you're thinking you *don't want* it. For example, if you're repeatedly thinking *I don't want to be late*, you're emitting the stressful, frantic energy of being late, and will doubtless be late. Instead you want to think calmly and confidently, along the lines of *I am always on time* or even, *I always reach my destination with time to spare.*

If you tell your partner or children, *I don't want to fight,* you're focusing on the fighting, which is what will continue to manifest, not the peace or cooperation you'd prefer. If you're always thinking *I can't cope with my huge workload*, the universe feels the energy of you having a massive amount of work and gives you more and more work than you can handle. Better to think *I get exactly the right amount of work for me to do with ease*, or any phrase more positive to declare to the universe what you *do* want, not what you *don't* want.

In the same way, it's better to be *for* something rather than *against* its opposite, as then you're focusing on whatever you do want, for example, peace, justice, clean air, rather than what you don't, such as war, inequality, pollution. Then the universe will match with its frequency the thoughts and visions you have of a better world and not keep repeating the same things you don't want.

Pay close attention to your thoughts about everything, especially the lesser liked things in your life, such as debt, job loss or relationship difficulties. Stop any thoughts if they're focused on the negative, forgive yourself for having such thoughts, and then pivot your thinking towards what you do want instead, by using the techniques on the following pages.

However, please don't get scared that all your negative thoughts and visions will play out. According to Michael B Beckwith, Founder of the Agape School of Consciousness, 'It's been scientifically proven that an affirmative thought is hundreds of times more powerful than a negative thought. That eliminates a degree of worry.'

Plus, there's a time delay between having thoughts and them manifesting. It takes time and conscious focus to make thoughts reality, but if you consistently think negative thoughts and feel low-frequency emotions over a period of time, your life will not be able to change for the better.

Make the decision now to stop downward-spiralling thoughts in their tracks. State that these are weak thoughts and that you only want to have powerful, positive ones from now on, to create the upbeat, exciting and fulfilling life of your dreams.

CHAPTER 3

Ensure success

YOU'VE SET YOUR intentions through repeating affirmations, and spend time every day visualizing your dream life, but there are other creative and fun exercises you can do to ensure success. The key to manifesting, after all, is to be having fun and enjoying life, so you're reaching and radiating higher frequencies of being, which attracts other high-vibe scenarios into your life. So undertake the following activities with a sense of openness, curiosity and playfulness.

ACT *AS IF*

Your thoughts and beliefs are revealed in your actions, but you can also reverse that and use your actions to change your beliefs. Try doing things that are just outside your comfort zone of usual behaviour and act *as if* the life of your dreams is already manifest. These new actions, if done regularly enough, lead to your old limiting beliefs breaking down and a new belief forming that allows your dream life to naturally unfold.

To overcome never having enough money, make a point of gifting – to charity or to friends – even if it's just a little more than you would normally give. Many faiths, such as Buddhism and Islam, know that giving money keeps the energy of prosperity flowing towards you. As you give, you will receive. Being generous with what you do have is an act of faith that more money will come to you. However, *do not* push yourself into debt with this act. It should make you feel a little uncomfortable, which is how you know you're going against your beliefs of lack, but don't recklessly give what you don't have and make yourself feel worse. Feel a sense of gratitude that you earn enough to help others, and trust that there will then be plenty for you. Also, try paying a bit more towards any bills or debts you owe. If you can sustain paying out a little extra every month, and do it with a feeling of abundance and joy that you're paying your debts down even more, then you will re-shape your belief around money, and more will come your way.

If you want a new romantic partner in your life, start to become aware of and practise all the things you'd do as a couple. Research romantic destinations to go to, book pairs of concert tickets, and buy small gifts of appreciation as if you have someone to give it to. Clear out space in your cupboards for them to put their things into when they move in with you, and buy yourself bunches of flowers as gifts from a 'secret admirer' as if you really had one. Don't let yourself feel sad that you haven't found a lover yet; all these actions should be done to uplift your energy and send a message to the universe that you are ready for that special person to come into your life by acting *as if* they're already there.

When you want a new home, as well as looking in estate agents' windows and browsing their websites for suitable properties, go on viewings to look around all the lovely places that catch your eye. Imagine yourself living there and how it would work with the rest of your life, envisioning the commute to work or the school run from that house. While you're waiting for the right home to come to you, have a good clear-out of anything you don't want to take to your new pad, as if you've bought it already. Clearing out the old is a great way to signal to the universe that you are ready to attract something new. Plus, you can start packing boxes of things you don't use every day, ready to move quickly and easily when you are ready.

If you want to travel around the world, get your passport sorted and start researching all the places you'd like to go. Read up on where you want to visit and start planning your trip – even if you haven't got the funds for it yet. Work out costings to go to certain places. Pack your suitcase. Print out pictures of all the locations you're going to visit and stick them up where you can see them every day at home. The key is to feel as if you've already booked the tickets and are heading out for the holiday of a lifetime.

Whatever it is you'd like to achieve, from a new job or car to a healthy body or spiritual enlightenment, think of ways you could act *as if* those desires had already happened. Start practising these actions daily, consistently, with genuine enjoyment and enthusiasm, and hijack your beliefs into making your dreams manifest.

CREATE A VISION BOARD

A vision board is a giant collage of photos and images of everything you want to bring into your life. Making one is a fun, creative activity to do to help you get clear on what you want to experience, have some attractive imagery to daydream from and connect you to Source, as any creative endeavour does.

Spend some time looking through magazines, catalogues or websites for the kind of things you'd like in your life. When you find the right picture of your dream car, photos of rooms in your dream home, perfect pet or any other material object you wish for, tear or print it out. This might include beautiful furniture, interior décor, plants, garden designs for your ultimate home, favourite fashions or places you'd love to visit around the world.

In the same way, search for imagery that depicts more conceptual aspects of your ideal lifestyle, such as happy friends, a loving partner or rich spiritual development. This could include photos of yoga retreats, smiling people all gathered around a table, a couple holding hands at sunset. You can include recent photos of happy times with friends or family, or places you've loved going to, to add some uplifting memories to the collage. Finally, print out a recent photo of yourself to place in the centre or at the top of the vision board. After all, this is about creating *your* best life.

When you've collected all the pictures you want, find a large piece of paper, to make a poster collage of all your chosen images. In the centre you could write an affirmation to attract all these desires to you, such as:

I am attracting my
dream life to me now.

I am manifesting my best
life.

I attract my dream life,
with joy and ease.

The universe is bringing
all I desire to me in
perfect timing.

Then arrange and glue all the different photos around the affirmation in a way that's pleasing to you. Enjoy this joyful creative process for what it is, making a beautiful collage of imagery that reflects your wildest dreams. Don't dwell on what you don't have, trust that these wishes will be fulfilled all in good time. Right now, you're getting really clear on what you want to ask the universe for to enable you to reach your highest potential.

When it's all finished and dry, stick your inspirational vision board up on your wall where you will see it every day and can imagine all those wonderful things and circumstances in your life now. Really feel the joy and fulfilment of all these things already being in your life. Keep your frequency high by focusing on all that you love to do and thinking only positive thoughts. Follow any inspiration to act on your desires in any small steps that bring them towards you. If you don't want to make a poster for your wall, you can do the same process to create a scrapbook of all your most dreamed-of desires.

Create an attractive cover with your photo and a powerful affirmation on the front. You could arrange all the images into categories of your life, such as health, career, relationships, and start each section with a different affirmation relevant to the images you place there.

With both creative practices, feel free to add anything else that makes you feel as if these wonderful life circumstances are already manifested, such as 'New Home' cards, 'Congratulations' messages for the new job, or a Valentine's Day card from your lover-to-be.

Look through your book of dreams every day, and allow the pictures to prompt creative visualizations and intensely evoke the happy feelings of everything you want manifesting in your life. Don't forget to update the content regularly as you receive the things you manifest and as new wishes take shape, changing want you want. This helps keep the visualizations based on the images fresh and exciting. Revitalizing the feelings you have for your desires will bring them closer to you.

Write yourself a cheque

A classic powerful manifestation secret, made famous by the actor Jim Carrey, is to write yourself a cheque, dated in the future, for the amount you desire by that time. Stick it onto your vision board or in your scrapbook, or anywhere where you will see it every day, and visualize how amazing you will feel to receive that money.

Carrey had just started acting when, in 1985, he wrote himself a cheque for $10 million for 'acting services rendered', dated 'Thanksgiving 1995'. He kept it in his wallet and looked at daily, imagining himself earning that amount of money. Incredibly, the day before his cheque was dated, he got the contract for *Dumb and Dumber*, for the fee of... ten million dollars!

TAKE INSPIRED ACTION – ONE STEP AT A TIME

One of the surest ways to manifest your dreams is if they are backed by inspiration and service to the highest good of all, including the highest expression of yourself. Wanting material things and personal experiences just to keep up with others or acquire as status symbols for appearance's sake is desiring out of fear. If you worry you won't be seen a certain way if you don't have something, or want a certain thing out of jealousy of others, for example, the motive behind your desires is not in alignment with the highest good, which is love or Source energy. When your dreams are in alignment with Source, you can relax and trust that they will manifest without you having to work too hard and push for them.

However, you do need to take action on your dreams and get started in some way as soon as you get the inspiration. Don't have a great idea to do something and sit on it, worrying about how it will turn out or fearing you won't reach your goal. Get started, in a small way, immediately! You don't need to know all the steps it's going to take to get to the end result, but you do have to take action towards making your desires a reality. Begin the book writing, painting or any other creative project you've always wanted to accomplish by doing it for just ten minutes when you first get the idea. Set a timer and do the activity for that time. The same goes for starting a new exercise regime or spiritual development activity; just do it for a short amount of time to start with. Chances are you'll get stuck into it, start enjoying it, and won't want to stop when the timer goes off. But if you do, that's fine, you've completed what you set out to do. You have started on the path to achieving what you want.

Don't get distracted or let other things get in the way of achieving your dream. Write it in your diary to do the same thing the next day, and every day, until you've written a whole chapter, then the book, painted a whole picture, or reached your desired weight. Make the small steps a daily habit, and eventually you will reach your goal. Keep in mind the end result, the joyous, celebratory feelings of accomplishment and pride, vibrant health and incredible wellbeing, and know that you are now on the way towards making these dreams a reality.

As Martin Luther King Jr is quoted as saying, 'Take the first step in faith. You don't have to see the whole staircase. Just take the first step.'

LEVEL UP YOUR EMOTIONS

Even when doing all these, simple, fun and exciting actions to help manifest our dreams, our emotions can still ebb and flow. Maintaining a positive vibration is key to ensuring success in manifesting, but it isn't always easy. Low mood can hit at any time, whether it's insecurity and self-pity from looking at social media for too long, anger or disappointment at someone else's or your own behaviour, or doubt and worry over the future. But if you can do or think something to boost your feelings even just a little bit up the following scale of emotions, as defined by Abraham-Hicks and shared in Gabrielle Bernstein's book *Super Attractor*, then you're on the way to feeling better, aligning more with Source and manifesting your dreams.

Acknowledge how you feel according to the scale below and see if you can move up a level or two. This isn't about dwelling on your emotions or glossing over them, but feeling them, releasing them safely by letting the tears flow, punching a pillow, or writing it all out, and then choosing to feel a better feeling further up the scale. Try to reach a higher state than the one you're in at any given moment (not necessarily *the* highest state of joy or love, as this might be too much of a leap) with the help of your thoughts or any actions that lift your mood enough to gain momentum in the right direction.

1. Joy / appreciation / empowerment / freedom / love are the highest-frequency feelings.

2. Passion, in what you're doing and / or what you're thinking about.

3. Happiness / eagerness / enthusiasm

4. Positive expectation / belief

5. Optimism

6. Hopefulness

7. Contentment

8. Boredom – see how high this is up the scale, and if you're at this level you just have to *do something you enjoy* to easily reach a better feeling.

9. Pessimism

10. Impatience / irritation / frustration

11. Feeling overwhelmed

12. Disappointment

13. Doubt

14. Worry

15. Blame

16. Discouragement

17. Anger – You might have thought this emotion would be lower on the scale, but with anger there is at least energy moving in your system. Even if it feels bad at the time, it can be released and transform your frequency for the better. But not if you feel the need for…

18. Revenge

19. Hatred / rage

20. Jealousy

21. Unworthiness / insecurity / guilt

22. Fear / grief / desperation / despair / powerlessness

If your feelings are still raw over a past event, take time to talk or write about it and release the emotions in a healthy way, from the safety of the present moment. Realize that this past trauma is no longer happening in the now, and you are safe and well in the present moment. Bringing your focus back to the present moment, by closing your eyes and taking a few deep, soothing breaths, for example, can really help shift perspective and move your mood up the chart.

Service serves you too

Doing something for someone else is a fantastic way to boost your emotions to a higher state and help someone else in the process. Phone a friend to see how they're doing, play a game or do an activity with your child, volunteer to walk a neighbour's dog. These activities take you out of your head, into the present moment and into service for others. They very quickly change the way you feel and can swiftly raise your frequency to a higher state.

CHAPTER 4

Notice wins

YOU'VE WORKED OUT what you truly desire and asked the universe for it in a variety of ways. Your daily practice includes saying positive affirmations, visualizing yourself celebrating and keeping your vibration high, as much as you can. When you think about what you want for your life, you feel excitement, exhilaration and passion about your new projects. You know that you deserve good things to happen to you and you trust that you will be shown the way forward. Now you just need to pay attention to the guidance, signs and synchronicities that are the universe's way of taking your hand and leading you towards your dreams.

SIGNS OF SUCCESS

Guidance comes both internally and externally. When you meditate you may get inspiring ideas for your next steps, either during or after sitting in stillness. You may receive messages from your inner self, your soul, from spirit guides or even from loved ones passed over. The more you tune into your inner wisdom, the more you will come to know how it communicates with you. It may be as simple as getting a strong urge to do something different that you know will help you progress towards your dreams. You may see images in your mind's eye showing you the way or, if your clairaudient skills are really attuned, you may even hear words of encouragement or get downloads of important information leading you towards your best self. Write any messages of guidance down as soon as you can, and read back later, sensing how to go about acting on them as soon as possible. When you act on guidance from Source energy in this way, it comes to meet you knowing you mean business, and that's when the magic unfolds.

Be open to noticing and responding to the often mind-blowing signs and synchronicities that help you know you're on the right path. You may doubt them initially because of their perfect timing or spot-on answer to your calls or queries, but they are what happens when you're in flow with the universe. Here are some magical moments to look out for:

* You meet exactly the right people to mentor you or work with you on your dream goals. Be open to even strangers

showing you the way, or the most unexpected scenario bringing you the best person.

★   Conversations with others will answer the very questions you have or point you to the next step of your journey. Pay close attention to everything said to you, or any messages that come from the radio or television, even in the form of songs or slogans.

★   Messages on billboards or on the side of a vehicle can be the sign you were looking for, if they are an answer to what you were thinking about just before you saw them. Don't ignore the seemingly bizarre signs aligning in perfect timing. They are still showing you that you're on track.

★   You may be drawn to look at a magazine, a noticeboard or a website and the exact article to help you is there. Maybe even a course or event you need to go to is happening soon, and you're free. Don't hesitate to book a place straight away.

★   Perhaps you're browsing in a bookshop and a particular book falls at your feet, and it's the perfect one to encourage you or give you more ideas about what you need to do next. Maybe it even lands open on a page with a profound message, perfect for you, as if guided by a spiritual force. Buy the book or take a photo of the page if you can.

★ If you go for a psychic or tarot reading, you will be given the exact advice and answers you need at that moment, deepening your certainty you're doing the right thing.

All of these events, and more, can happen to you when you simply relax and allow life to unfold in the direction of your dreams. There are countless stories of such 'coincidences' occurring at exactly the right time that they cannot be mere chance. Start writing yours down in a synchronicity journal, as the more you notice them, the more often they will occur to steer you on your path. Trust it's the universe working on your behalf and answering your requests to manifest your desires. Celebrate, act upon the guidance and follow wherever it leads.

TEST YOUR POWERS

Practise your basic powers of manifestation by thinking about something you feel fairly neutral about, that you don't have strong feelings for or against. Let's say it's fish. Think about fish as much as you can throughout one day. Meditate on fish. Visualize fish whenever you can. Then stop, and just see how many fish appear in your reality from then on. Chances are, they will appear everywhere, in designs on crockery, stationery or clothes, on car bumper stickers and posters, actual live ones in rivers and lakes, on special offer at the shops. This shows that we create our reality according to what we think about, and should empower you to focus on what you do want.

START SMALL

It's perfectly understandable to want the five-bedroom house with ten acres of land, a swimming pool and tennis courts, but a part of you might not believe it's possible straight away, especially if you're currently living in a bedsit with minimal income. To avoid being disheartened when such grand dreams don't manifest straight away, scale your desires down to more realistic aspirations to begin with. You can still have and do all the incredible things you really desire, but if it feels a tad overwhelming to achieve the mightiest of your wishes, right now, aim for less and then go bigger when you see the power of attraction working and believe in it more.

Try starting your manifestation journey by asking the universe for something small, such as a parking space right near your work, or an available table at your favourite coffee shop. Here's how to get started:

* Powerfully intend to attract the desired thing to you.

* Affirm it happening by stating *I attract the most perfect parking space [or whatever small goal you want to happen] now.*

* See it appearing exactly where and when you want it.

* Feel how great it will feel.

★ Believe it will happen, thank the universe beforehand, and watch it manifest.

From these smaller creations, you will gain the confidence to enable you to attract the bigger requests in your life.

SET A DAILY DESIRE

You could set a goal for the day and watch it manifest. Pick something that you believe can happen, but equally may not. Maybe you'd like to finish or start a certain project, or receive some money out of the blue. You might want to hear from a particular friend, get a lovely compliment from someone or a bunch of flowers from your lover.

* Start by sitting quietly, focusing only on breathing in and out.

* When your mind and body are still, talk clearly with the universe about what it is you want.

* Give your reasons why, exploring how reasonable it is to want it and what it would mean to you to have that happen, today.

* Trust the universe has heard your request and will grant it.

* Now, in your mind, really see an image of that desire playing out exactly as you wish. Feel how fantastic it will be to manifest this, today.

When your daily goal occurs, take the time to celebrate it. Give yourself credit for creating exactly what you wanted in your life. Equally, if it doesn't work out, don't ditch the desire altogether. Take responsibility for improving your manifestation muscles. Refine your request, sharpen your focus, improve your visualization – and try again tomorrow!

GRATITUDE IS THE KEY

'Wear gratitude like a cloak and it will colour every area of your life,' wrote Rumi, the 13th-century Persian poet and Sufi mystic.

All the New Thought experts, from William Clement Stone in the early 1900s to contemporary manifestation expert Gabrielle Bernstein, know that practising gratitude is one of the major keys to achieving your dreams. Being thankful for your blessings tunes your awareness into all the wonderful things, people and experiences in your life, which lifts your mood and, therefore, raises your vibration, attracting more high-vibe circumstances to be grateful for.

As spiritual psychologist Teal Swan says in her YouTube video on raising your frequency, 'Looking at things with an attitude of gratitude is in alignment with pure source energy – it is an exact match to the highest frequency there is: unconditional love.' If you're resonating at the level of pure love, you'll receive that energy back tenfold. Plus, being in a state of appreciation creates an energy of acceptance of the way things are and means you're not in resistance to what may come. It enables you to relax and trust that more good will come.

Oprah believes that, 'Grace is a direct response to gratitude. The more gratitude you have, the more grace steps in and shows itself and mirrors that gratitude.' As per the law of attraction, whatever you focus on with love and appreciation for it being in your life, will expand and grow into even greater manifestations.

Sometimes, when things go wrong, we can get into a bad habit of focusing on and complaining about the negative aspects of our life. But this only drags us down further and can attract more undesired circumstances. Far better to tune in to what is going well, as opposed to what's not working, even if it's just the little things that make you smile or feel good during the day. Maybe you have a loving pet and appreciate them snuggling up to you on the sofa or feel grateful you were able to make yourself a delicious, nutritious lunch and felt fantastic after eating it. Choose to make a habit of appreciating the good stuff going on in your life. It will make you feel better, lift your energy and reinforce your awareness of the true abundance in the world. Then you can open your mind and your heart, once again, to the loving flow of the universe bringing your desires to you.

CREATE A GRATITUDE JOURNAL

A wonderful way to make gratitude a daily practice is to have a gratitude journal. In a pretty notebook, perhaps with a beautiful photo or pertinent affirmation on the front, spend time writing down all the things you appreciate in your life already. This can include everything from waking up in a warm, comfortable bed and being able to have a good stretch on your yoga mat every morning, to having enough money to feed your family and time with a much-loved friend. It might be as simple as feeling grateful for your breath, or as complex as your career path.

Start with ten points of appreciation every morning, and really feel how each one uplifts your energy. You can even go on a 'rampage of appreciation' as Abraham-Hicks calls it, thinking about and appreciating more and more things in your life, from the big to the small, the general to the specific, really feeling the joyful energy your appreciation creates inside you. Meditate more on these nourishing feelings of gratitude until you're positively vibrating with the love of the universe at all the wonderful aspects of living. Imagine it rippling out into the world until you're grateful for everything on the planet. As hard as it may seem initially, even the crises, disappointments and people you don't get on with can be appreciated, as they are still teaching you something about yourself in your journey towards being your most self-aware best. Be grateful for how far you've come, and where you are, right now, as it's on the path to where you want to go.

Every evening, before you go to sleep, jot down five specific things that you feel grateful for that happened during the day, such as a happy conversation with a pal, a great workout, a lovely meal or cup of coffee, the sun on your face as you sat outside watching the birds and butterflies. Going to sleep with your frequency at a blissfully high vibration of gratitude and love not only means a better night's rest, but also means you start the next day without resistance to attracting more good experiences into your life.

You can cultivate an 'attitude of gratitude' at many other times throughout the day by slowing down any task or activity, becoming deeply present with everything you are doing and giving thanks as follows:

★   When having a bath or shower, feel grateful for having hot
    water plumbed into your home, for the bathroom, the soap and
    shampoo, and the fact you have the money for it all. As you
    wash yourself, focus on every part of your body from your head
    to your toes, and deeply appreciate all that each bit does for
    you every day. You can do the same appreciation ritual as you
    dry yourself or when you rub moisturizer into your skin, really
    giving your whole self some love and appreciation.

★   When exercising, walking or dancing, give thanks for having
    the health and vitality to be able to move in such a way. Turn

your attention inside your body to all the miraculous organs performing their various important functions. Say how much you are thankful for your perfect, healthy heart, lungs, liver, eyes, ears, hands, and so on.

★ Every meal time or even when simply having a cup of tea or coffee, think about all the people and processes involved in making your food or drink and give thanks to the farmers and produce-pickers, the truck drivers and the shop keepers who helped bring it all to you. Thank the food itself, the seasons for cultivating crops and Mother Earth for creating such a plentiful bounty of nourishment for us to thrive on.

★ Make a point of telling loved ones how grateful you are to have them in your life. As you talk with them, listen deeply and look at them with pure love and appreciation. Share with them the specific qualities that you most admire and feel blessed to have the benefit of. If a friend or family member live far away, why not write them a letter or text message of pure appreciation? Sending your gratitude out in this way is a powerful frequency raiser for you both. Imagine how special and loved it will make them feel, not to mention how good you'll feel thinking of all the ways they help, support or make you smile.

Another way in which to use gratitude to manifest is to give thanks for the things you want to receive as if they're already in your life. Saying, *I am blessed with ... an abundant income / fun-loving and supportive friends / an exciting, generous lover,* or whatever it is you're wanting to attract, is a great way to bring it into being. Every day, say out loud, *thank you, thank you, thank you for giving me good health, abundant wealth, wonderful friends and laughter* and feel the joy and gratitude that this will bring, knowing it is coming to you with this practice.

You don't even have to be specific to manifest a magical life. Regularly stating *I am so blessed* or *I love my amazing life full of wonderful surprises,* and really feeling genuine love and appreciation for your life, is enough for the universe to respond by creating scenarios to give you those very feelings.

Appreciate the people in your life

If you've fallen out with a friend or been badly hurt by a lover or family member, try this technique to manifest a better relationship. On a piece of paper, list everything you appreciate about that person. This can be extremely challenging if you still feel pain over what happened, or if resentment has built up over the years, in which case write down all that you've learned from the relationship, such as standing up for yourself more or setting stronger boundaries. The aim of this task is to let appreciation and even forgiveness come in to release your feelings of anger, betrayal or disappointment. Then you can release the energetic hold that person has over you, which is blocking better relationships and the abundance of the universe from fully making its way to you.

CELEBRATE EVERY SUCCESSFUL MANIFESTATION

Whenever your desires start manifesting, whether dreamed about long ago or wished for just that morning, remember to take some time to give heartfelt thanks. Notice even the small indications that you're beginning to create what you want in your life, such as the perfect parking space or interesting job ad. Spend a couple of minutes in reverence and appreciation for what you wanted coming into being, thanks to the universe co-creating it with you.

Don't let the voice of fear creep in to sabotage your manifestation. It may suggest that things are 'too good to be true', fill you with worries about it all going wrong or doubt that you can handle it. Stop this resistance to what's meant for you by immediately going big on appreciation. Celebrate that you created this thing or circumstance you desired – along with the universe's help, of course! Feel all the feelings of delight, amazement, jubilation and awe in yourself and your powerful creation abilities. Write down in your gratitude journal the moment the law of attraction really worked for you, describe how it happened and how incredible it feels. Consciously staying in a positive frame of mind about your miraculous manifestations means you can ride on the elevated energy to the next incredible creation, fully enjoying the adventure as it unfolds.

CHAPTER 5

Overcoming challenges

DESPITE FOLLOWING ALL the previous guidance, manifesting might not always go according to plan. You may experience blocks, such as doubt and resistance, stopping your dreams coming into reality as soon or as smoothly as you'd like. Sometimes, no matter how much you are visualizing and affirming the desired positive outcomes, the same negative situations keep manifesting. So what's happening to hold up your best life manifesting, and how can you overcome the challenges that get in the way?

Firstly, it's important to acknowledge and accept whatever's happening to stall our dreams. While the law of attraction is all about reaching for ever greater feelings of happiness, when life gets tough it is far better to be fully present with the negative feelings as they arise, rather than deny and bury them. Until lower-vibration emotions are expressed, safely, they will stay in your system and attract more negative thoughts, feelings and scenarios. Sit with whatever feelings are rising to the surface, feel and express them fully, by crying for as long as you need to, angrily punching a pillow or writing all the blame, shame, guilt or fear down until you feel like you've reached a release of the emotions, or hit on deeper issues to work on for resolution.

WORRY AND FEAR

Fear – of failure, change, loss, or something else – can really stand in the way of you fulfilling your desires. Teal Swan, in her YouTube video *How to Stop Expecting the Worst (Catastrophizing)*, suggests the following exercise of writing down your deepest fears to be able to move past them.

* Go to the worst-case scenario in your mind and feel all the feelings connected to it. This way you're facing your fears head-on rather than worrying about them, which is stuck resistance energy and needs to be released through fully acknowledging the worst.

* Look at all your fears and divide them into two groups: those that you can do something about, the others that you can't.

* For those you can do something about, write a plan of action steps to help you move beyond them. Just taking small steps to bust through your fears shows you that you're capable of more than you realized.

* For those fears you can't prevent, try to find some things that make you feel better about them. For example, if you worry about having a car or plane crash, research their safety so you can realize your fears are statistically unlikely to ever happen.

★   If you feel it would help gain some more perspective on your worries, take an inventory of all the times when you coped with any calamitous events in your life, when you were brave, strong and fully capable of dealing with whatever 'bad' thing happened. Maybe it wasn't as horrendous as you had feared or it actually all worked out well in the end. Perhaps it was even for the greater good or a higher purpose that the undesired outcome occurred in the first place.

Worrying about something bad happening does not necessarily make that thing manifest. Swan explains that studies show that 40 percent of what we worry about never happens, and 30 percent already has happened, which you can't change, so why waste time worrying about the past? Some 22 percent of our anxieties are over things that a change in perspective or better planning can improve, this includes worrying what others think about you (it's none of your business so drop it!), being late or what to wear (spend time planning the route or outfit well in advance). This leaves just 8 percent of what we worry about that actually happens. Of these events, 4 percent are out of our control, such as natural disasters or accidents, so 4 percent of our worries are within our control, things that we could have been more prepared for or planned accordingly so they didn't happen, or simply been fully present enough at the time to know what to do and be able to act fast enough to stop that event unfolding.

As mentioned in the previous chapter, the best way to stop worrying is to start appreciating. So as soon as you start to fret over anything, instead feel grateful for all the things and events that have manifested without drama in your life, the people that help and support you, the joyful moments you have experienced without any hiccups or harm. Keep writing down the signs and synchronicities that show you that the universe is on your side and wants good things to happen for you. When you see this as the truth of existence, and start to trust in the benevolent power of the universe or Source energy, you can even hand over any worries directly to this higher power. If you're having difficulties with a relationship, for example, whenever you start to go over what happened in your mind and worry about it never being resolved, simply state, *I hand over my relationship grievances to the universe. I trust that a higher power is working to bring peace and happiness back to my partnerships.* You can then imagine all worry floating away to be taken care of by the universe, Source or God. Visualize and feel how lovely that connection is now everything has been cleared up and rectified. You deserve fully loving, supportive relationships that bring peace, joy and fun to your life. Affirm this often and it will be so.

The more you connect with the spiritual realm through awareness, meditation and other spiritual practices, the more reassurance it can give you in times of trouble. If you know that beyond the trials and tribulations of your life there is greater power working for the good of all, then you come to trust that all really will work out well. When the woes of the world are getting you down and global events seem too much to cope with, connect, via the breath, to the calm stillness within you. Stopping any stresses and stories in your mind to meditate brings you closer to the vast consciousness unifying all things, to the great oneness of all of life, where the manifestation of your best self, living your best life, is waiting to materialize.

VICTIMHOOD

Sometimes, when things seem to be going wrong, it can be a way of experiencing what you *don't* want so you can more accurately know what you *do* want. Part of living a life as a soul in a human body on this planet is to sort through the contrast of your experience to discover what is not wanted and go in the direction of what is wanted. A negative, even traumatic, experience might be something your soul has called in for you to go through to help you get really clear on exactly what it is you desire. Such events give you the chance to pivot more clearly towards what you do want to manifest and how you want to feel. Aim to see unfavourable events in this light, instead of wallowing in self-pity or victimhood, which are further blocks to manifesting good in your life.

Pay close attention to what you think and how you talk, all day long. If you often complain, blame, or feel sorry for yourself, you're living in a state of victimhood and this will always disempower you and keep you from achieving your dreams. As soon as you notice yourself thinking in this way, think a new thought to re-train your brain to react differently. Simply state: *I am learning new ways to think about my life, now. All is well.* This stops your usual thinking and opens your mind to something new and transformative.

Remind yourself that life is full of challenge; it's part of the journey. But staying attached to dramas creates turmoil in your reality and is unlikely to be the truth of where you are, in the here and now. When you stop the ego running amok with past or future scenarios and drop any upsetting narratives from your mind, you will most likely find that, in this very moment, all is indeed well. Focus on getting really present by taking one slow, deep breath at a time, or by becoming deeply mindful of what's going on around you, right now, via your senses. See the leaves of a tree blowing in the wind, feel the air on your face, smell the cut grass in the garden. From this present moment of grounded stillness and calm, you can relax and allow your desires to manifest.

If you still find yourself in the same unwanted, unpleasant and upsetting scenarios in your life, the same patterns repeating over and over, it can be frustrating and seem as if the universe is not listening to what you want. But, explains Swan, it's trying to help you get there by giving you the same situation in order for you to make a different choice, to think, say, decide or act in a new way and change the pattern, once and for all. The best way to discover the change you need to make when faced with the same experience again is to ask the question *what does the universe want me to do differently this time?* It may take a lot of self-enquiry via focused reflection or therapy, but once you realize how you need to be different, and act on it, you will receive a situation reflecting that change for the better.

LIMITING BELIEFS

Another aspect of your thought patterns that can stall your manifestation process is having limiting beliefs that clash with the mindset needed to make your dreams reality. Our parents or guardians, plus the culture and era we are born into, shape our beliefs in our early years around love, happiness and prosperity. For example, you may have come from a poor background where it was a struggle to pay the bills. This would create a fundamental belief in lack, in there not being enough for everyone, which makes it harder to believe that total abundance is available for everyone and feeling good is your birthright. Contrary to what you might have experienced and therefore believe, you do not have to work hard to create prosperity in your life, be 'perfect' at whatever you do or live a life of selfless service to others to 'deserve' a good life.

Many people with strict parents or religious upbringings that see God as an external authority figure, judging every action, find it hard to believe in the benevolent, expansive energy behind all of existence that wants you to be and have all you desire. When love is withheld if you are 'bad' and only given to you if you are deemed 'good', you feel you have to earn everything in your life by being perfect, selfless and hardworking. With this early punishment and reward programming, you're likely to criticize and judge yourself harshly, regardless of what you do, let alone if you feel you've made 'mistakes'. Deep down you believe you are not worthy or not good enough and, therefore, undeserving of all the good you want to manifest.

But you are worthy of everything you want, purely by being a fragment of Source energy in human form having those desires. You deserve all that you wish for, simply because you dream of having or experiencing it, not because you have done all the right things to be rewarded. Say often: *I am worthy of everything I desire.* You can have whatever you want as soon as you turn your attention towards it, rather than towards the lack of it. The universe does not judge or doubt you, and it never withholds anything that you want. You just get in the way with your self-hate and limiting beliefs, which are out of alignment with Source, as this is the energy of love and abundance. When you are in alignment with Source, coming from a place of self-love, your desires are already yours waiting to come into form through your thoughts, words and actions. Once they are created in your mind, through imagination and intention, they are either resisted or allowed to come into being, when you are the vibrational match for all the love, happiness, fulfilment and success you wish for.

RESISTANCE

Resistance is an oppositional force that suggests you're out of alignment with something or someone, or even parts of yourself. It can come from inside you, from your thoughts, words and actions holding you back from your highest self and desires by making you anxious, fearful or depressed. Or it can come from outside, from others who might not want you to change or from external events thwarting your progress in a certain area.

When you are working on raising your vibration, certain circumstances and people may not be in alignment with your energy anymore. As we shift our frequency, we may no longer want to do the things we once did, such as going out drinking all evening or gossiping and complaining about others, as these things will drag our vibration down. Friends, family or our partner may resist how we're changing. Explain that you are on a path of spiritual development and your values and priorities have changed, but you still want to spend time with them doing different things. Either they will be up for trying new activities with you, happy that you are following your joy, or you will end up seeing that person less and less, until perhaps the relationship ends altogether. As sad as this may be, it is a part of the manifestation process, whereby only those in alignment with your highest desires will stick around. Why would you want anyone in your life stopping you from attaining your dreams anyway?

We can be resistant to things or people that would be good for us, as well as to that which we should avoid. Resistance exists for a good reason and is always valid, as a sign that something needs examining before moving forward – or not. If you feel resistance to anything or anyone, address it before making a decision or taking any action. Otherwise, as many law of attraction experts agree, *what we resist persists*, as we are still focusing on it and confirming it in our reality.

Internal resistance can be a warning sign that something isn't right for you, or that habitual negative thought patterns and behaviours are blocking you and need exploring and working through. For example, you may say you want to get fitter and lose weight, but have opposing thoughts about finding it hard to shed those extra pounds. You may decide you want to stay sober, but then resist this decision by getting drunk. Resistant actions only lead to more suffering, feeling as if we're betraying ourselves, in a never-ending cycle of resisting what is good for us.

Get to the root cause of any resistance to feeling better and living the life of your dreams by being curious about where this resistance comes from. Be gentle and compassionate with yourself, but take some time for deep introspection and questioning, journalling or even therapy to resolve the conflict within you. If you feel yourself put the brakes on something, unable to get fully on board with a plan, a project, relationship or activity, look honestly into why you feel resistant. Be especially vigilant of any excuses to stop you examining your deeper truths, as we can even be resistant to healing, living in denial that anything is wrong because facing the truth can be painful. But if you face and resolve any resistance, then every part of you will be moving in the same direction towards your goals and they will manifest much quicker and easier.

If you still can't seem to get to the root of why you feel resistance, you can always offer up your struggle to Source for help. Gabrielle Bernstein suggests saying:

I recognize that I'm out of alignment with [name the person, situation, belief system you're resisting]. I choose to release the outcome and feel good now. Thank you, Universe, for guiding me.

DOUBT

When whatever you want doesn't appear to be manifesting as quickly or in the way you have planned, it can be easy to doubt the process and lose faith in your co-creative abilities. But once you start doubting, more doubtful thoughts enter your head and you will quickly block your dreams from appearing. This is the moment to stay strong in your belief that all will manifest in good time. Practise infinite patience and trust in the universe's divine timing. Reassure yourself by stating as many times as you need:

I know I am receiving all I desire now.

Once you've formed your visions and desires, believed in them coming true and started taking action steps towards them, it's only a matter of time before your thoughts become things. But it can take a while to turn your life around when forming new beliefs and getting to the root of resistance. Don't put unnecessary pressure onto yourself to reach certain goals within particular timeframes, and start to think it's not working or you're not doing it right. Relax more into the present moment, trust everything will happen when the time is right, and continue to pay close attention to all the wonderful aspects already in your world. Rather than dwelling on your dreams, do things that make you happy, in the now, and appreciate the many small pleasures in your everyday life. Then your manifestations will be even closer to becoming reality.

CHAPTER 6

Everyday magic

WHEN YOU START to work with the law of attraction every day, so that the techniques described in this book become a habit, then you will experience the incredible magic of a life lived 'on purpose'. This means that instead of creating your life by default, going wherever the wind blows, and then complaining that wasn't the right direction, you have to be deliberate about what you think, say and do to be the best version of yourself and manifest your best life.

CREATE YOUR DAY IN ADVANCE

As well as starting your day full of appreciation for what's already in your life and affirming all you want to manifest, you can consciously create your whole day in advance by thinking about what you want to happen, down to the last detail.

One of the early New Thought writers of the late 1800s, Prentice Mulford, even knew that, 'When you say to yourself, "I am going to have a pleasant visit or pleasant journey," you are literally sending elements and forces ahead of your body that will arrange things to make your visit or journey pleasant.' So always begin your day with an expression of gratitude for all that is to come. Breathe in deeply, smile, and when you breathe out say: *Today is a wonderful day, full of wonderful experiences.*

Then, instead of rushing into your day, take some time to think about what you have planned and visualize it going well. Create your life intentionally by thinking, seeing and feeling everything you want to happen each day working out well in your mind, body and spirit. Imagine a swift, smooth commute to work, see smiling faces and warm greetings at the meetings you have, feel yourself pleased that you started or completed a project. And if you have nothing in particular planned for today, imagine a wonderful surprise coming your way and stay open to all opportunities.

Design your day around doing things that feel good to you, whether it's walking your dog, seeing a friend, eating a delicious treat, seeing a movie or planting your garden. Know that you are consciously taking control of your life and placing things in it that make you happy and keep your vibration high, to do over the next day, week or month. This active scheduling will help you avoid any worry or catastrophizing about what's to come, because you'll know that much of it is going to feel good, boost your mood and raise your vibration to enable you to attract even more delight into your life.

Whatever you'd like to happen to enhance your wellbeing, try visualizing it for five minutes every morning and really feel the emotions of it coming to fruition. It can be as huge as healing the rift between you and a sibling, in which case you must feel the relief of a conversation going well, understanding being reached and a get-together being planned. Or it might be something seemingly simple but just as life-changing as having more fun and laughter in your life. For a noticeable boost to your mood, imagine yourself belly laughing, tears streaming down your cheeks with mirth. Do this every day for two weeks, and watch as hilarious situations happen right in front of you, your colleagues keep cracking jokes or a new television series makes you guffaw with glee. Finding the funny side in life is a major frequency-raiser and an important key to manifesting anything.

SIMPLIFY YOUR LIFE

'Be a curator of your life,' says author and *Zen Habits* blogger Leo Babauta, by consciously choosing the experiences you want to have each and every day. 'Slowly cut things out until you're only left with what you love, with what's necessary, with what makes you happy,' he recommends.

Make deliberate choices of what you want to focus on and accomplish each 24 hours you have, but do not overload your schedule too much. By clearing the unnecessary and uninteresting things from our day, we realize we can focus on what really matters to us and what brings us most bliss. Many hugely successful leaders in their fields, such as Tiger Woods and Elon Musk, recommend picking one passion, one project only, and directing all your intentions and actions towards that one thing being the best it can be through all your manifesting effort. Narrowing our focus can lead to excellence in one area, and free up more time to relax and enjoy life.

Babauta's book *The Power of Less* extols the many benefits of simplifying our lives so we have more time to be and appreciate every moment, not fill up all our time with more doing and accumulating. Life is happier, he says, when we scale down our demands on it and enjoy what we have, not rush through life ticking off everything on our to-do list.

'We're so caught up in trying to do everything, experience all the essential things, not miss out on anything important,' he says, but, 'We can't read all the good books, watch all the good films, go to all the best cities in the world, try all the best restaurants, meet all the great people. Life is better when we don't try to do everything. Learn to enjoy the slice of life you experience, and life turns out to be wonderful.'

The more you simplify your life down to all that you really want, the happier you will be. Here are some tips to help:

★ Declutter your home of everything you no longer need and that doesn't bring you joy. Sell things or give them away to friends or to charity.

★ Make fewer commitments to events that you're not fully enthusiastic about. It's okay not to say yes to every invitation.

★ Pull back from social media. Post and scroll less, live more.

★ Think hard about which relationships you can also pull back from. If anyone is draining your energy when you're with them or think about them, that's a big clue. Can that relationship evolve with you? What do you need most from your closest friends? Don't feel you 'should' stay in touch. Only ask, *do I want to?*

★ Slow down and focus on one task at a time.

★ Think less, meditate more.

RE-IMAGINE YOUR DAY

If, for whatever reason, some things haven't gone quite the way you had planned, you can always re-imagine your day so they went well. In Rhonda Byrne's book *The Secret,* the teacher Neville Goddard shares his wisdom called 'The Pruning Shears of Revision'. He recommends going over specific events or conversations in your mind, at the end of the day, and replaying them in a way that makes you feel better. You may wonder what the point is, if they have already passed, but by imagining such events going exactly as you'd wished, you are clearing up your frequency from the day and sending forth a new positive vibration for the next day. Instead of focusing on any mistakes, consciously create new images of the future, so things go better next time.

LIVING IN UNCONDITIONAL LOVE

A powerful way to elevate your life even more, according to Wayne Dyer in his book *Manifest Your Destiny*, is to live as unconditional love. Not the romantic or familial love that we're all capable of, but a heightened state of being. Go about your day with a sense of yourself as a part of the benevolent, creative, flowing consciousness, pure Source energy, that you are. It is not an easy task, as our ego mind always wants to chip in with commentary on this person or that event, and about yourself. But make a promise to yourself to try, for a day, a week, or longer if you enjoy it, to only allow unconditionally loving, gentle and kind thoughts to come from your mind, and actions to flow from your heart. Vow to become more of the God-force within you by making a practice of unconditional love.

By emanating this loving energy into your environment, through your thoughts, words and actions, responding in a new way to life, you will find people around you reacting differently to you, too. As a spark of Source practising unconditional love, you allow everyone and everything to unfold naturally, just as flowers and plants do. Do not judge anything, whether good or bad, as everything is part of the one great consciousness and is allowed to expand as it desires. This doesn't mean that you accept aggression or

unpleasantness, but you see that the spirit beyond the behaviour is the same as your spirit, and all are a part of Source.

In your meditation practice, focus on your own unconditional loving heart energy as a bright ball of white light in the centre of your chest. Feel its deeply loving essence dissolve any judgement, anger or hatred in you. See this ball of pure loving consciousness growing bigger and brighter. Radiate it outwards into your home, community and the world. Sit in that sense of bliss for as long as you wish (not forgetting to bring all your energy back in again afterwards and send away any that isn't yours, to clear your energy field).

Beam love ahead of you every day to set the tone for what's to come. Send it into every situation you find yourself in, or think about, such as upsetting world events. Pour love into every person you come across, regardless of whether they're a close companion or a despicable political figure. Do this daily and you will find your relationships deepen spiritually, you will sleep better, have more energy and feel more at peace much of the time. Not only this, but you will begin to notice your life filling with more joyful synchronicities leading you to your dreams and clarifying your purpose, which is ultimately to love more.

How to live in unconditional love

✦ Choose to tune into love in every moment throughout the day. Just like you tune your radio to a certain frequency, tune yourself to the frequency of loving consciousness. In any circumstance, ask yourself: *What would love do here?*

✦ When you meditate, or at any time of the day when you feel overwhelmed or stressed, make a habit of inhaling unconditional love and exhaling fear.

This includes letting go of anxiety about making mistakes, your appearance, how you are seen by others. It's all fear and not love. Feel it leaving your body every time you breathe out, allowing only divine love to be breathed back in. Notice how this relaxes you into trusting the universe.

◇ Take a big breath in and say or think of unconditional love. *Breathing in unconditional love.*

◇ Breath out nice and long, and let go of all fear. *Breathing out fear.*

✦ See only the positive everywhere you go and stop judging others. When you're out walking or driving somewhere, decide to look for things that make you feel good when you look at them. It can be anything from flowers blooming by the roadside to a child and parent holding hands happily, a dog running with joy towards its owner, or friends warmly embracing. Noticing more of the love in your environment will bring even more of that love into your world.

✦ With a partner of your choice, pick a day to both only practise unconditional love. Make sure everything you do, say and think is infused with only love. If you find yourself complaining, preaching, judging, worrying, catch yourself and switch to thinking and radiating only love. After 24 hours, report back to each other about how it went, and if you started to feel more happiness and peace in your life, carry on for another day or more.

✦ Allow others in your life to do their thing without any comment, criticism or even help from you. For example, if your children are squabbling and you usually step in, hang back and say, lovingly, 'I see you are having difficulty getting on. I trust you to work it out and be friends again.' Usually when we get out of others' way, they rise to the challenge and learn more from it than when we step in to adjudicate.

✦ Hand any difficult situations that you have been struggling with over to Source by asking for divine guidance to help and to be shown the way forward with unconditional love. It's ok to admit you don't know what to do and ask a higher power to assist. Follow the urges and signs showing the way to peace. When help appears, remember to give thanks.

CONCLUSION

No limits to life

ABOVE ALL, MANIFESTING is all about feeling good – every day, in the moment, as well as in your dream life in the future. It's about living in love, with a constant connection to the great oneness binding all life together. It's about appreciating what's around you every day, seeing joy everywhere and finding your own ways to keep your frequency high. You need to find out what you love to do and do it as much as you can, really letting your passion and enthusiasm for whatever it is fill your being and boost your energy.

If ever you don't feel your best, really explore why, as growing self-awareness is also part of the expansion of consciousness that's in the process of becoming. Work on releasing any painful feelings, and then do something, anything, to raise your vibration. Never forget the incredible transformational potential of music, movement and appreciation to instantly improve your mood. If in doubt or still feeling down, drop everything and meditate, as this unites you with the deep stillness, the oneness, the God force or Source energy that all things are made of and from which everything manifests.

The journey towards fulfilment will still feature challenges and setbacks, but it will also include a lot of fun, hope, promise, excitement and adventure. Try to see any obstacles as gifts to help you understand yourself better and get clearer on what you want, via what you don't want. Learn from the past, then let it go. Don't look back, face forwards into the future, where new opportunities will present themselves. Don't worry about the destination, apart from to see and feel yourself laughing, smiling, celebrating whatever the wins may be.

Stay curious and open to learning more about yourself and work on revising your own perceptions. You are a being of infinite potential, a spark of Source having a human experience. Shed all expectations of how things 'should' be in every area of your life. Preconceived ideas limit your experience and take away from the joy and the beauty of what *is*. Make time to really look around and see how magical and rich life is. Without limitations, anything is possible. Dream your best life into being and raise the vibration of all humanity, living in unconditional love and abundance.

INDEX

FURTHER READING

BOOKS

Ask and It Is Given by Esther and Jerry Hicks (Hay House, 2004)

Becoming Supernatural by Dr Joe Dispenza (Hay House, 2017)

The Biology of Belief by Bruce Lipton PhD (Hay House, 2011)

Excuses Begone! by Wayne W Dyer (Hay House, 2009)

Infinite Possibilities by Mike Dooley (Beyond Books, 2019)

Manifest Your Destiny by Wayne W Dyer (Element, 1997)

The Magic of Manifesting by Ryuu Shinohara (Self-published, 2019)

The Power of Now by Eckhart Tolle (Yellow Kite, 2001)

The Secret by Rhonda Byrne (Simon and Schuster, 2006)

The Spontaneous Healing of Belief by Greg Braden (Hay House, 2009)

Super Attractor by Gabrielle Bernstein (Hay House, 2019)

You Can Heal Your Life by Louise Hay (Hay House, 1984, 1987, 2004, 2005)

ONLINE RESOURCES

www.abraham-hicks.com

www.gabbybernstein.com

www.thelawofattraction.com

www.leeharrisenergy.com

www.tealswan.com

Do You See the Signs of the Universe by Ulla Suokko | TEDxBigSky on YouTube